Dominick Argento
Six Elizabethan Songs

BOOSEY & HAWKES

AN IMAGEM COMPANY

DISTRIBUTED BY

HAL•LEONARD®
CORPORATION
7777 W. BLUEMOUND RD. P.O. BOX 13819 MILWAUKEE, WI 53213

www.boosey.com
www.halleonard.com

DOMINICK ARGENTO

Dominick Argento, considered to be America's pre-eminent composer of lyric opera, was born in York, Pennsylvania in 1927. At Peabody Conservatory, where he earned his Bachelor's and Master's degrees, his teachers included Nicholas Nabokov, Henry Cowell, and Hugo Weisgall. Argento received his Ph.D. from the Eastman School of Music, where he studied with Alan Hovhaness and Howard Hanson. Fulbright and Guggenheim Fellowships allowed him to study in Italy with Luigi Dallapiccola and to complete his first opera, *Colonel Jonathan the Saint*. Following his Fulbright, Argento became music director of Hilltop Opera in Baltimore, and taught theory and composition at the Eastman School. In 1958, he joined the faculty of the Department of Music at the University of Minnesota, where he taught until 1997. He now holds the rank of Professor Emeritus.

Although Argento's instrumental works have received consistent praise, the great majority of his music is vocal, whether in operatic, choral, or solo context. This emphasis on the human voice is a facet of the powerful dramatic impulse that drives nearly all of his music, both instrumental and vocal. Writer Heidi Waleson has described Argento's work as "richly melodic... [his] pieces are built with wit and passion, and always with the dramatic shape and color that make them theater. They speak to the heart."

During his years at Eastman, Argento composed his opera, *The Boor* (1957), which has remained in the repertoire; John Rockwell of *The New York Times*, writing of a 1985 production, stated that "[it] taps deep currents of sentiment and passion." Following his arrival in Minnesota, the composer accepted a number of commissions from significant organizations in his adopted state. Among these were the Saint Paul Chamber Orchestra, who commissioned his suite *Royal Invitation* (1964); and the Civic Orchestra of Minneapolis, who commissioned *Variations for Orchestra [The Mask of Night]* (1965). Argento's close association with Sir Tyrone Guthrie and Douglas Campbell, directors of the Minnesota Theatre Company led to his composing incidental music for several Guthrie productions, as well as a ballad opera, *The Shoemaker's Holiday* (1967).

The 1970s and 1980s saw the composer working increasingly in the song cycle form, while still writing operas and orchestral music. Among his major song cycles are: *Letters from Composers* (1968); *To Be Sung Upon the Water* (1973); *From the Diary of Virginia Woolf* (1975); *The Andrée Expedition* (1982); and *Casa Guidi* (1983). Two further song cycles, both premiered in 1996, are *A Few Words about Chekhov* (mezzo-soprano, baritone, and piano), given its premiere by Frederica von Stade, Håkan Hagegård, and accompanist Martin Katz at the Ordway Theater in St. Paul; and *Miss Manners on Music*, to texts by the noted advice columnist.

Since the early 1970s the composer's operas, which have always found success in the U.S., have been heard with increasing frequency abroad. Nearly all of them, beginning with *Postcard from Morocco* (1971), have had at least one European production. Among these are *The Voyage of Edgar Allan Poe* (1976), *Miss Havisham's Wedding Night* (1981), and *Casanova's Homecoming* (1984); Robert Jacobson of *Opera News* described the latter work as "a masterpiece." *The Aspern Papers* was given its premiere by Dallas Opera in November 1988 to great acclaim, was telecast on the PBS series Great Performances, and was again presented, to critical praise, by the Washington Opera in 1990. It since has been heard in Germany and in Sweden; June 1998 brought a performance at the Barbican Center in London.

Dominick Argento examined fame and the immigrant experience in *The Dream of Valentino*, set in the early days of Hollywood. Washington Opera gave the work its premiere under the baton of Christopher Keene in January 1994, followed by its co-commissioning company, Dallas Opera, in 1995. The production featured special multi-media sets by John Conklin and costumes by the couturier Valentino. Writing of the premiere, Peter G. Davis of *New York* magazine stated, "What a pleasure to encounter a real opera composer, one who has studied and learned from his predecessors, loves the form, understands its conventions, has mastered them, and then lets his imagination take wing." *The Dream of Valentino* received its European premiere in February 1999 in Kassel, Germany.

Among other honors and awards, Dominick Argento has received the Pulitzer Prize for Music, given in 1975 for his song cycle *From the Diary of Virginia Woolf*. He received the 2004 Grammy for "Best Classical Contemporary Composition," awarded for Frederica von Stade's recording of *Casa Guidi* on the Reference Records label. He was elected to the American Academy of Arts and Letters in 1979, and in 1997 was honored with the title of Composer Laureate to the Minnesota Orchestra, a lifetime appointment. He was the recipient of the 2006 World of Song Award, granted by the Lotte Lehmann Foundation.

In honor of his 85th birthday, the University of Maryland presented a special career restropective that included *Miss Havisham's Fire*, *Postcard from Morocco*, and *Miss Manners on Music*, as well as other recitals and lectures.

CONTENTS

SIX ELIZABETHAN SONGS

Pianist on the Recording: Laura Ward

The price of this publication includes access to companion recorded accompaniments online,
for download or streaming, using the unique code found on the title page.
Visit www.halleonard.com/mylibrary and enter the access code.

SIX ELIZABETHAN SONGS

Six songs for high voice and piano, composed 1957–58 (scored for baroque ensemble in 1963)
19 minutes
Poetry by William Shakespeare, Ben Jonson, and others
Piano version first performed 23 April 1958, Eastman School of Music, Rochester, New York;
Nicholas DiVirgilio, tenor; David Burge, pianist
Baroque ensemble version first performed 8 March 1963, First Unitarian Society, Minneapolis, Minnesota;
Carolyn Bailey, soprano; George Houle, oboe; Jane Burris, harpsichord; Jane LaBerge, violin;
David Ferguson, cello

Composer's Comments

The two years at Eastman plus the following one abroad were the happiest and most fulfilling years of my life. When I graduated Bernard Rogers said, "Dominick, you're one student I won't worry about. I'm sure you'll make it." I was still an unknown composer, but my confidence had increased greatly, and I now had an exclusive contract with Boosey & Hawkes, the publisher of Strauss, Bartók, Stravinsky, and Britten. To top it off, I had been awarded a Guggenheim Fellowship. Not surprisingly, we opted to go to Florence.

After touring England, France, Holland, Germany, and Switzerland, we moved into a fine apartment in Florence in a little park along the Arno at Lungarno Torrigiani 7, a block east of the Ponte Vecchio. Little did we know that the following four Florentine apartments we'd occupy over the next forty years would all be within a block of the Ponte Vecchio. I settled down to begin work on my first full-length opera. Around Christmas we had a letter from Nicholas DiVirgilio, a friend and fellow student at Eastman who had sung the tenor role in the premiere of *The Boor*. He wanted me to write some songs for his graduation recital. I went to the bookstore on via Tornabuoni, and from the limited number of volumes of English poetry they had, I bought a copy of Francis Palgrave's *The Golden Treasury* and chose a group of six poems of the Elizabethan era to set. Our apartment had a wonderful view, but the heating left much to be desired: the room where we had placed the piano had none at all. That winter I wore mittens at the piano and could see my breath as I tried out the phrases of these songs...

The *Elizabethan Songs*—the very first work I composed upon finishing graduate school—has turned out to be my most performed piece. At present there are at least seven recordings (four American, one English, one German, and one Australian), several of them done with the baroque ensemble arrangement (which I prefer) instead of the original piano accompaniment. It shows up frequently on recitals and seems to be a favorite with voice teachers. Once, during a three-day residency at a University of Wisconsin campus, I was asked to coach voice students working on my songs. At least thirty of them brought in the *Elizabethan Songs*. All but a couple of the singers had photocopies of the music: the two or three printed scores in evidence were library copies. Afterward I described my amusement to Stuart Pope, my publisher at Boosey & Hawkes. "I don't see anything funny about that," he huffed. "You should have refused to coach 'em!"

Excerpted, with the cooperation of the composer/author, from
Catalogue Raisonné As Memoir: A Composer's Life
by Dominick Argento
Published by the University of Minnesota Press
© 2004 by Dominick Argento
Used by permission

For Nicholas Di Virgilio

I. Spring

original key

THOMAS NASH

DOMINICK ARGENTO

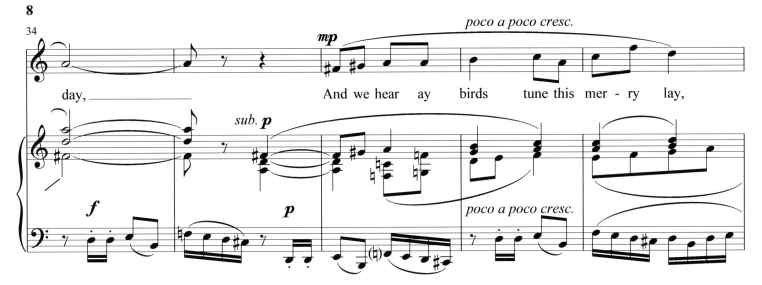

day, _____ And we hear ay birds tune this mer - ry lay,

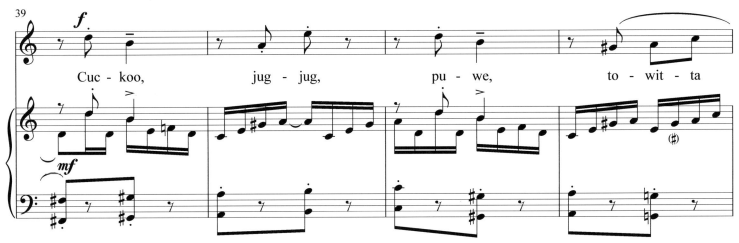

Cuc - koo, jug - jug, pu - we, to - wit ta

woo! _____ The fields breathe sweet,

the dai - sies kiss our feet, Young lov - ers meet, old wives a- sun - ning

II. Sleep

original key

SAMUEL DANIEL

III. Winter

original key

WILLIAM SHAKESPEARE

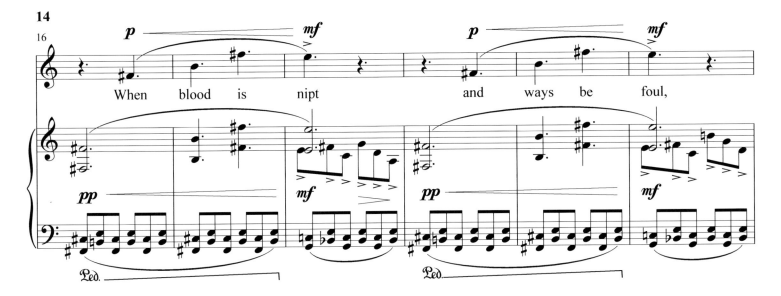

When blood is nipt and ways be foul,

Then night-ly sings the star-ing owl _____ Tu - whoo! Tu - whit!

Tu - whoo! _____

A mer-ry note! _____

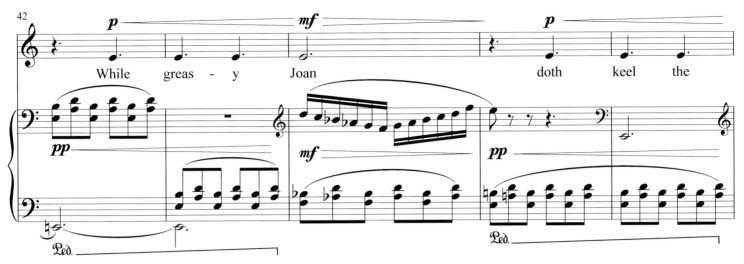

While greas - y Joan doth keel the

pot

When all a - loud the wind doth blow, _____ And cough-ing

drowns the par - son's saw, _____ And birds sit brood-ing in the

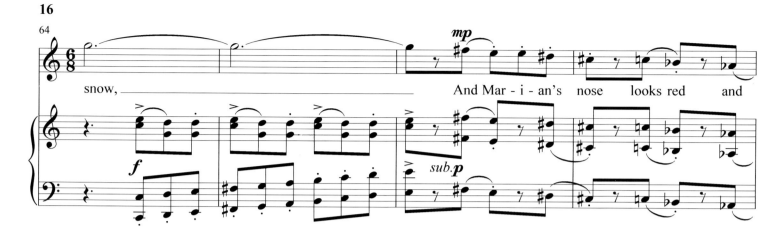

snow, _____ And Mar - i - an's nose looks red and

raw; _____ When roast - ed crabs

hiss in the bowl Then night - ly sings the star - ing

owl _____ Tu - whoo! Tu - whit!

IV. Dirge

original key

WILLIAM SHAKESPEARE

20

V. Diaphenia

original key

HENRY CONSTABLE

Di-a-phen-i-a, like the daf-fa-down-dil-ly, _____ White as the sun, fair as the

lil - y, _____ Heigh ho, how I do love thee! _____

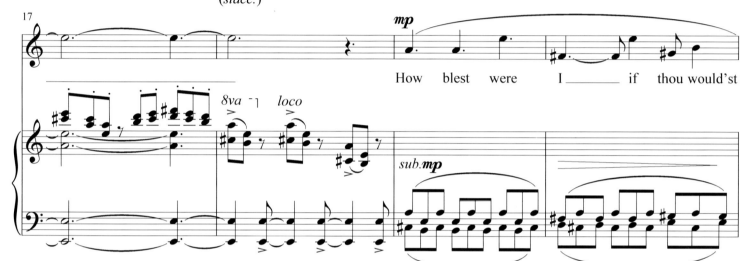

Fair sweet, how I do love thee! I do

love thee as each flower loves the sun's live-giv-ing power;

For dead,

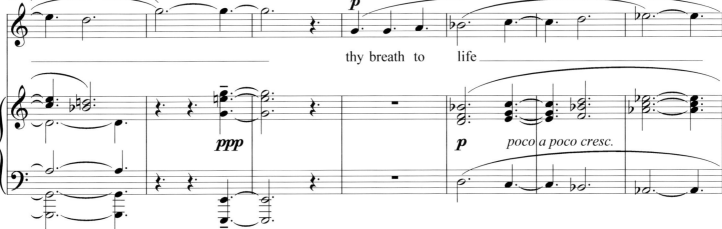

thy breath to life

might _____ move me. _____

Di-a-

phen-i-a   like to all _ things bless-ed _____   When all thy prais - es _____   are _ ex press - ed _____

Dear   joy,   how I do love   thee! _____   As   the

VI. Hymn

original key

BEN JONSON

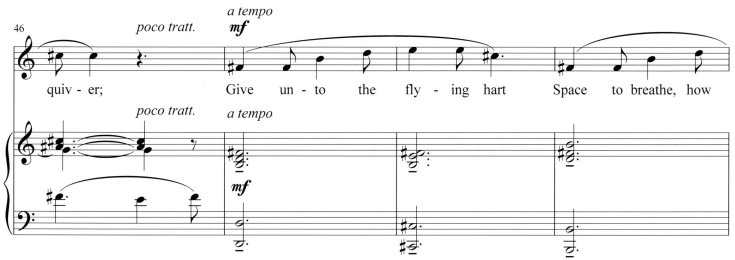

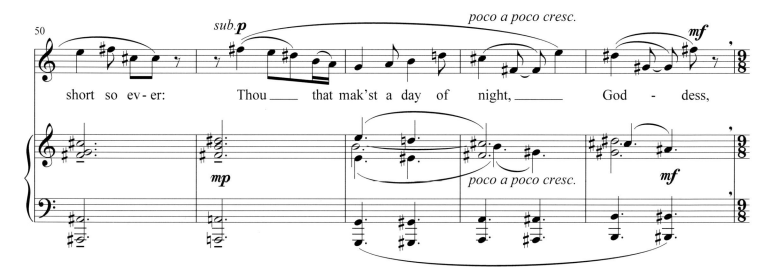

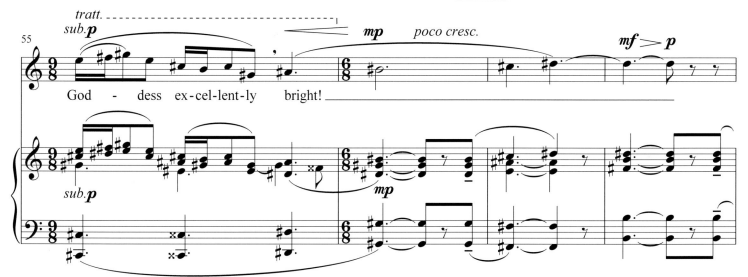